MAYIBUYE

25 Years of Democracy in South Africa
LAWRENCE MDUDUZI NDLOVU

African Perspectives Publishing
PO Box 95342, Grant Park 2051, South Africa www.africanperspectives.co.za

ISBN PRINT 978-1-990931-23-9
ISBN DIGITAL 978-1-990931-29-1
Typesetting: Gaynor Paynter
Cover image by Mfundo Mthiyane
Editing: Raphael d'Abdon

Contents

For the living-dead:

Ngudle Solwandle, Mampe Bellington, Tyita James, Salojee, Suliman Gaga Ngeni, Hoye Pongolosha, Hamakwayo James, Shonyeka, Hangula Pin, Leong Madiba, Alpheus Tubukwa, Jundea Kgoathe, Nicodemus Modipane, Solomon Lenkoe, James Mayekiso, Caleb Shivute Michael Monakgotla, Jacob Haroon, Abdullah (Imam) Cuthsela, Mthayeni Timol Ahmed, Mdluli Joseph, Tshwane William, Mohapi Mapetla, Mazwembe Luke, Mbatha Dumisani, Mogatusi Fenuel, Mashabane Jacob, Mzolo Edward, Mamashila Ernest, Mosala Tebalo, Tshazibane Wellington, Botha George, Ndzanga Lawrence, Ntshuntsha Nanaotha, Malele Elmon, Mabelane Mathews, Joyi Twasifeni, Malinga Samuel, Khoza Aaron, Mabija Phakamile, Loza Elijah, Haffejee Hoosen (Dr), Mzizi Bayempin, Biko Steve, Malaza Sipho, Tabalaza Lungile, Ndzumo Saul, Mgqweto Manana, Muofhe Tshifhiwa, Aggett Neil (Dr), Dipale Ernest, Mndawe Simon, Malatji Paris, Tshikudo Samuel, Sipele Mxolisi, Mthethwa Ephraim, Raditsela Andries, Ndondo Batandwa, Kutumela Makompe Nchabaleng Peter, Jacobs Xoliso, Marule Simon, Mashoke Benedict, Mntonga Eric, Bani Nobandla, Zokwe Sithembele, Makaleng Alfred, Sithole Clayton Sizwe, Tlhotlhomisang Lucas, Madisha Donald Thabela, Vuyisile Mini, Frederick John Harris, Mthuli ka Shezi, Rick Turner, Clemens Kapuuo, Solomon Mahlangu, David Sibeko, Griffiths Mxenge, Neil Aggett, Ruth First, Vernon Nkadimeng, Thamsanga Mnyele, Victoria Mxenge, Benjamin Moloise, Andrew Zondo, Immanuel Shifidi, Dulcie September, David Webster, Anton Lubowski, Abithur Albie M. Abrahams John, Albert Gama, Alpheus Dlamini, Anthony James, Baepi Sanny, Baker Lewis, Baloi Robert, Baloyi Jacob N. Bandon Gordon, Bantwini N. Basset Basel, Bawo-Dlamini Albert, Beck Godfrey K. Bengu Dumisane, Bennun Tollie, Bhedava John, Bhentele Nimrod, Bhongo Khululani, Bileya Philimon, Biza Toto, Bonya Lulamile, Bookolane Thabang, Boshomane Abel, Bosigo Mompati Godfrey, Botha Zanethemba Michael, Bucibo Joyce, Buthelezi Duncan, Buthelezi Gcina, Campbell John Ralph, Campoi Siabilelo, Ceku Mvula, Cele Ndose Paul, Chauke

vi

Ditshabako, Chauke Elijah, Chiliza Tsitze Chimane Loate, Choncho Sibusiso, Cothoza June Rose Nontsikelelo, Dadoo Winnie, Dadoo Yusuf, Daka Mandla Henson, Trevor Huddleston, Robert Sobukwe, Lilian Ngoyi, Oliver Tambo, Adelaide Tambo, Govern Mbeki, Nelson Mandela, Winnie Madikizela-Mandela, Sr Bernard Ncube, Archbishop Dennis Hurley, Mendi Msimang, Manto Tshabalala-Msimang, Billy Molise, Jonny Makhathini, Robert Sobukwe, Chief Albert Luthuli, Sol Plaatje, Pixley ka Isaka Seme, Dalamba Siseko, Dali Sureboy, Dalinyebo Sabato, Daman Ceaser T. Damane Bimmy Caeser, Daniel Molokisi, Dantile Lulamile H. Daries Glen, Davids Ephraim Ivan Adam, Deyi Gladman, Dikeledi Paul, Dimba Themba Francis, Dinonyane David, Dintsi Samson Isaac, Dintsi Simon, Ditshabako Brenda, Dladla Jackson, Dladla Mzala, Dlamini David, Dlamini Douglas, Dlamini Fikile, Dlamini Gangamshini, Dlamini George Perm, Dlamini Johannes, Dlamini Mavela, Dlamini Mzanempi, Dlamini Patrick, Dlamini Sekby, Dlamini Sithembile, Dlodlo Theophilus, Dludla Reginald, Dlwathi Siphiwe, Dube John, Dube Lesley, Dube Moses Sesulu, Dubula Isaac, Dude Lesley, Duma Gcina, Duma Martine, Dumela David, Dyani Lizethile, Dywili Mfundo, Olof Palme, Walter Sisulu, Albertina Sisulu, Nomaka Epainette Mbeki, Z K Matthews, Edward Lawrence, Eliana Gertz, Essop Yunus Ahmed, Faku Thabile, Fazzie Mzwandile, February Basil, Feni Dumile, Festinstein H. Fihla Thamsanqa, Fineberg Danny, First Julius, First Ruth, First Tilly, Fish Gustin, Flatela Kgotso, Frans Mawethu D. Funani, Mangaliso Oscar Orlando, Futhane Mzala, Gabela D. Boy, Gaetsewe Jon T. Gagarin Boston, Galela Champion, Gama Albert, Gazongo James M. Gcina Mziwoxolo, Geer Ahmed Mohamed, Gerald Ganyqaza, Gnqose Daphne, Godolozi Qaqawuli, Goldberg Annie, Goniwe Jacques, Gova Zwelindaba, Govers Harry, Gqabi Joe Nzinga, Gqirana Mobbs, Guma Mduduzi, Gxekani Mzwandile, Habase Andile, Hamlyn Michael Frank, Harmel Michael, Hashe Govan Mantyi, Hashe Sipho, Henne Zingisile, Hlatshqayo Machocho, Hlatswayo Hlatswayo, Hlekani Gandi, Hlobo Mziwoxolo, Hlongwane B. Sydney, Hlongwane Nelson, Hlongwani Vuyani, Hlophe Joseph Arsenius, Hodgson Percy John, Hoyi Cekiso, Ilane Patrick, Jabanje Levy Tebejane, Jack Musutabantu, Jack

Samukele, Jacob Padi, Jele Rueben Mandla, Jezile Phillip, Jona Zakhele, Jones Hekelia Mark, Joseph Zami, Joyce Thoby Steven, Kaloli Thamsanga, Kana Samson N. Karabo Freda, Katz Freda, Keke Steven, Kelly Mzolisi, Kesupile Galdys Kelape, Ketani Stanley, Kgejane Andries M. Kgobe Jacob, Kgori Bennedict, Kgozi Benedict, Khalima Maritsane Lukas, Khan Sam, Hector Peterson, Khanyile William, Khaya Major, Khayiyane Sipho, Khethelo Johannes, Khosi David, Khoza James, Khumalo Florence, Khumalo Philip, Khumalo Sithembile, T. Khumalo Vikeliswe Colin, Khutho Ngwane M.E., Khuzwayo Dingane, Khuzwayo Irvin, Khuzwayo Sibusiso, Klaas Jan, Knight James, Kobole Euginia Kakale, Korjas Peter, Kotane Moses, Kozi Hoshe, Kuboni Mvuleni J. Kutwana Abraham, La Guma Alex, Lafasi Clifford Nqaba, Lailaje Charles, Langa Christopher Nzimeni, Langa Vincent, Lawrence Edward, Leballo Boithlomo Derrick, Lebele Frank, Lebelwane Barney, Lebese Michael, Lebo Ena, Lekele Peter, Leshoro Robert, Lesia Ephraim, Lethuso Doctor, Letladi Patrick, Letuku Nathanial, Levinson Mankankaza, Lewatle Pope, Liphoko Patrick D. Lloyd Candi, Lokwanye Nujoma Tolbert, Lolwane Sidwell, Lubepe Francis, Lubisi Andy, Lungiso Musi, Luthuli Mphathi P., Luxomo Mthuinzi, Lwana Meshak, Mabaso Alan K., Mabaso Daniel Crosby, Mabaso Ndlovunga Sithole Jacob, Mabatla David, T. Mabhida Moses, M. Mabitse Patrick, Maboee Eleanor, Mabukane Ntobeko, Mabuza Thoko, Mabuse Simon Paul, Mabuza Leonard, Mabuza Reginald, Macamba Pasqual, Macfadden Keith, Machobane Themba Duke, Madakeni Leon, Madi Andrew, Madiba Aaron, Madimola Rethabile Patricia, Madingwane Stephen, Madondo Ronald, Madontsela Skhumbuzo, Mafika Stanley, Maga Eric, Magaga Bongani, Magagula Mgqibelo Frans, Magashule Sefelaro, Magekaza Mazizi, Magome David, Magqwashane Ernest, Magubane Bheki, Magxala Themba, Mahamba Sparks, Mahlakola Philemon A., Mahlangu Ben Vusi, Mahlangu Solomon, Mahle Thabo, Ahmed Kathrada, Mahlobo Mandla, Mahutso Solomon Albert, Majane Andrew, Majola John, Majola Leocadia Lungi, Makae Samuel, Makaheni Leon, Makalipha Theo, Makau Patrick M., Make Cassius, Make Dairaley, Makeni Jola, Makgale Ephraim, Makgotsi Jones, Makhalabeni

Vincent Kgasago, Makhasane Thabo, Makhathini Johnstone, Makhayo Autonio, Makhubela Lukas, Makhubelo Lucas, Makhubu Lawrence, Maki Nosisi Cecilia, Makopane Duluza Niel, Makudubethe Thabo, Makume Samuel, Malangabi Nonkululeko, Malati Chico, Malaza Josep, Malaza Sipho N. Malebane Pule Moses, Malebu Thobela, Maleka Kagiso Jeremia, Maleke Nikita John, Maloko Bernard, Maloma Tony, Malope Edward, Malotoane Martha, Maluleka Jubilee, Maluleka Robert, Malunga Reuben, Mamabolo Pamela, Mamba Mlamli, Mampuru Christopher, Mampuru Elijah, Manaka Sabata, Mandlenkosi Sifiso, Maneli Bob, Mangana Nelson, Mangana Tebogo, Mangean Phillip, Mankayi Lungile, Manona Monde, Manong Philly, Manzezulu Sheila Kukie, Manzini Christinah, Manzini Xoliswa, Mapelo Joseph, Maphalala Mowa, Maphetho Moses, Maphosa Absalom, Maphumula Shadrack, Maphumulo Reginald, Mapua Ronald M. Mapua Tiro, Maqhekeza Ngubekhaya, Maqolo Beauty, Marayi Lepota, Marks J.B., Marks Norman Patrick, Marwanqana Alfred F. Marwanqana Mzukisi, Marwanqana Thandi, Maseko Don Donga, Maseko Freddy, Maseko Isaac, Maseko Scelo, Maseku Abraham, Maseku Sophia Theko, Masemi James, Masemola Sandy, Masenoli Teboho Benny, Maserole Peter, Mashaya Solomon, Mashego Flag, Mashika King George, Mashini Duncan, Mashini Kenneth, Mashinini Paul, Mashlasela Otto, Mashobane Derrick, Masilela Grace, Massina Leslie, Masinga Vusumuzi, Masipa Barry, Masoje Johannes, Masondo Cecilia, Masondo Jacob, Masuku Sibusiso, Masupha Rocky, Matake Samuel,Matela Walter, Mathe Joel Jabulane, Mathe Vivian, Mathee V. Stanley, Mathi M. David Tshehla, Matiwane Mduduzi David, Matlala George, Matlou Johnny, Matomela Patrick, Matshoge Abraham, Matthews Boiki Mogorosi, Matya Siphiwe, Mavuso Babili, Mavuso Morris Mncube, Maweni Dumile, May Andile, May Aspin, Mayaka Ndumiso, Mayoli Joseph M. Mayona Sydwell, Mazenzo Sipho, Mazibuko Isaac Melusi, Mazibuko Mandla, Mazibuko Pappie, Mazibuko Themba, Mbali Jackson, Mbali Mxolisi, Mbatha Marg, Mbatha Mxolisi, Mbatha Sabelo T., Mbatha Sam, Mbaule Raymond, Mbele Masechaba, Mbele Stanza S., Mbele Thabo, Mbonambi Leslie, Mbongwe Emily, Mchunu

Sipho, Mchunu Victor, Mdingi Mnceisi, Mdlankomo Liqwa, Mdletshe Aubrey Sipho, Medupi Staloko, Melani Lenon, Meyer Leon, Mgaga Sika, Mgomezulu Gordon, Mgudlana Thafeni Wilton, Mgudlwa Mackay Davashe, Mgwacela Badman, Mhambi Charles, Mhlebeya Mfana Lamock, Mhlongo John, Mhlongo Reginald Enock, Mike Colenso, Mini Nomkhosi, Mira Bulumko, Miya Matthews, Mjovane Malixole, Mokgotsi Motsei, Mkhaba William, Mkhabela Kholisile, Mkhize Nkosikhona, Mkhize Simphiwe, Mkhize Thami, Mkhonto Mendo, Mkhonza Zelani, Mkhonzi Zakithi, Mkhwanazi Eric, Mkondo Polly, Mlandu Mandla, Mlangeni Johannes, Mlenze Michael, Mlindazwe Thamsanqa, Mlotshwa Bokale, Mmotha Nlwaitsile, Mmultane Matthew B. Mmultane Matthew M. Mncedisi Mdunga, Mngadi Mandla, Mngadi Vincent, Mnisi Donald, Mnyele Harry Thamsanga, Moabi Justice, Mochous Anita Mojabeng, Modimeng Joyce, Modisane Jerry, Modise Majoba, Modise Peter, Modise Tshepo, Modumo Ernest, Moegabudi Sam, Moeketsi Bruce, Moeketsi Sylvester, Moekoena Titus, Moemibi Sello Osborne, Mofaka Peter Kamohelo, Mofokeng Ali, Mogojane Albert, Mogopodi Abraham, Mogotsi Disani, Mohautse Lebaka, Mohlabane Josiah, Mohlala Caesar, Mohlala Daniel, Mojalefa Solomon, Mojapelo Ethel, Mokatsane Oupa, Mokgabundi Motso Mokgabudi, Mokgale Lentsoe, Mokgatle Maggie, Mokgoate Abel, Mokgobu David Lehlohonolo, Mokgothu A.K. Mokhebe Regina, Mokhele Trevor, Mokodutho Daniel, Mokoena Charles Mokoena, Mokoena Joseph Moeketsi, Mokoena Thabo, Molakoane Piet, Molale Kate, Molani Bolosha, Molefe Arios, Molefe Buti, Molefe David, Molefe M. Samuel, Molefe Popo D., Molefe Stanley, Molejane Daniel T., Moleko Marks Daddy, Molete Sakie, Moletsane Andrew, Moloi Oupa, Moloi Sparks, Moloi Thapelo, Molokwane Jacob, Moloto Daniel, Moloto Daniel Mabola, Moloto Ivy, Monametsi Dada, Monamoli Buki France, Monare Malani, Monase Boy Lelele, Mongale Lucky, Monoto Joy, Montshioa Matlaku, Monyane Matlala, Moodley Vernon, Mophosho Florence, Mophuthing Joseph, Morabe Mosele Eunice, Morake Simon, Morapedi Shadrack, Moreng Oupa, Moroalo Mzimkhulu, Morokane Morokane, Moropa Sydney, Morton Peter Wouter,

Mosagale Koboatau, Mosala Ernest, Mosala Patrick, Mosedi Patrick, Moses Myeza, Moshoeu Paki Gabriel, Mosia Aaron, Mosia Michael, Mosimane Butiki A. Mosimane Johannes, Mosupye Fitzgerald, Motane Lawrence, Motau Peter Sello, Motau Samuel, Motaung Lawrence, Motaung Tiger, Moteka Godfrey, Mothibe Christopher, Motladi Masere, Motlauthi Zaba, Motolo Carnot, Motsai Nocholas, Motsepe Joseph, Motsoasila Isaac, Motsoenang Ernest, Motsuenyane Sandy, Motswane Jackson Jones, Moutsusi Pelokgale, Mphahla Jomo, Mphale Morgan, Mphuthi Majoro Benedict, Mpongoshe Phakamile, Mshupa Ramokoti, Msibi Mandla, Msima Joseph T. Msima Msele, Msimang Shaka, Msimang Tyson Sibusiso, Msizi Harold, Msomi Dumisani, Msomi Mildred, Msweli Pashe, Mthandela Dumisane, Mthembu Charity, Mthembu Debra, Mthembu Joseph Boxer, Mthembu Thomas, Mtherreva Joseph Sparks, Mthethu C.N., Mthethwa Joseph, Mthethwa Paulos, Mothibe Caleb, Mothibeli Samson, Mthimkulu Richman Wandile, Mthubi Theodore, Mthusi George, Mtimkulu Siphiwo, Mtshali Khanyisile, Mtsweni Dick Nkukwana, Munisi Lentikile Magome, Musutabantu Jack, Muthupi Tshonoko, Mutlane Bob, Mvala Mark, Mvela Allen, Mvelo Cyprian, Mvemve Jimmy, Mvemve Adolf, Mvemve Boy, Mvevane Phako, Mzamo Namhla, Mzati Kenneth, Mziba Shadrack, Mzilikazi Gladman, Mzinyathi Monty, Mzobe David, Mzukisi Skweyiya, Naicker M.P. Naidoo Balakrishna Ramalu, Naidoo H.A. Naidoo Lennie, Naidoo Sahdhan, Nala Borne Jericho, Nala Linda, Nangu Billy, Nannin Billy, Ncube Linda, Ndabe Solly K., Ndebele Lucky, Ndlela Nhlanhla Cosmos, Ndlovu Brenda, Peter Mokaba, Ndlovu George, Ndlovu Goodwin, Ndlovu John, Ndlovu Joseph, Ndlovu Joseph Spoe, Ndlovu Monde, Ndlovu Sithembiso, Ndlovu Thrush, Ndluvu Mbuyiseli, Nduku Knox, Nduna Eric, Ndungane James, Ndwane Lungile, Ndwashlana Duduzile, Nene Thulani, Ngalo Ben, Ngasi Kholisile, Ngcobo Ezrom, Ngcobo Nkosinathi, Ngcobo Solly, Ngcobo Steven, Ngedesha Mongale, Ngele Selby, Ngema Pascal, Ngema Sipho, Ngesi Themba, Ngityane Simphiwe M., Ngobese Humphrey, Ngomane Macmillan, Ngon Mbulelo, Ngubane Daniel, Ngubane Jones, Ngubane Mazwi, Ngwema Vusumuzi Justice,

Ngwenya Johannes, Ngxito Cecil P., Nhlapo James B., Nhlapo Kenneth, Njaba Zoro, Njobe Mwelase Xola, Nkabinde Elias, Nkabinde Simion, Nkadimeng Elija Mandela, Nkadimeng Vernon, Nkilash Shani, Nkolonga Daniel, Nkomo Bongani, Nkondo Boetie Ephraim, Nkondo Victor G. Nkonjiwa Solomzi Simon, Nkosana Robert, Nkosi, Johannes Nkowana Sonny, Nkula Hector, Nkuna Styles, Nkutha Khehla, Nkutha Prisca, Nokwe Duma, Nondulo Ernest, Nonduwa Mzikayise, Nonelikana Samson, Nontshingala Nyameko, Norshee Sandile, Notana Sipho, Nqaba Gordon, Nqaphayi Shirley, Nqini Zola, Nqose Themba, Ntakwende Leslie, Nteyi Andile, Ntila Mike, Ntile Colenso Mike, Ntini Humphrey, Ntoyi Faku C. Ntshangane Elliot, Ntsibande Petrus, Nxumalo Mdu, Nxumalo Sifiso Howard, Nxumalo Victor, Nyanda Zwelake, Nyangiwe Sithembiso, Nyide Eugene, Nyoka Makhosi, Nyoni Willie, Nyukile Trom, Nzaba Zorro, Nzama Bazile, Nzima Jabu Nyawose, Nzima Patrick Boy, Oliphant David, Ondala Irvin Vusimuzi, Pama Sisa, Patrick Timothy, Peterson Michael, Phahle Cecil George. Phahle Lindie, Phakani Boykie, Phakathi Lucas, Phakathi Pascal, Phakathi September, Phako Mary, Phala George, Phalane Patrick, Pharasi Israel, Phillips James, Phinda Samual, Phiri Joseph, Pholosi Ethel Junior Pinki, Phosa Moses, Phunga Kid, Phungulwa Zenzile, Pieterson Joseph, Pindiwe Steven, Pindiwe Vicker, Pitso James, Pitso Sello, Plaatjie Maxwell, Polokela Matsela, Poo Mike, Preston Billy, Pule James, Pule Saskin, Pule Steve, Quin Jackie, Qupe Nceba M., Rabilall Krishna, Rabkin David, Rabkin Gerald, Radebe Jabu, Radebe Lancelot Manfuthi, Radebe Moses, Radebe Thandwefika, Rampela Joe, Ramsdale Eddie, Ramusi Selaelo, Rantao Christinah, Rantau Christopher, Rantokoana Humphrey, Rantokoana Jackson, Rasecho Alias, Rasetshu Elias, Ratsilane Amos, Ratsoma Modikane France, Resha Robert, Rosenburg Issy, Routh Guy, Schoon Jeanette Eva, Schoon Katryn Joyce, Sebugudi Ntrouko, Sechai Johannes, Sehularo Isaac, Sekele Peter, Sekulu Walter, Seleka Takatso Douglas, Selepe Donald, Selomo Ray, Sembeya Vorster, Senamela Themba, Senatla Tsotsi Samson, Seperepere Mamping, September Peter, Seremane K. Timothy, Seroto Matikwane, Sethilo Albert, Sethole Khulekane Innocent, Seti Gladstone, Setiko Patrick,

Setsoba Charles, Shabalala Amos, Shabang Hlapang, Shabangu Mandla, Shabangu Portia, Shandu Thabani, Shangase Absolom, Shangase Nomava, Shangase Thami, Shange Jerry, Shange Wiseman, Sharp Alfred, Shelembe Oscar, Shezi Mandla, Shezi Thando, Sibande Gert Richard, Sibande Peter, Sibanyone Ben, Sibanyoni Diagon-Roderick, Sibanyoni Rodrigues, Sibisi Jabulani Joseph, Sibonyoni Delmas, Simelane Ray, Sipho Vllakazi, Siramane Phillip, Sishi Jabulani, Sithole Ambrose, Sithole Arthur, Sithole Jacob, Sithole James, Sithole Peter, Siza Benny, Skhosana Mzwakhe, Skweyiya Singingo W. Sodere Ndumiso C., Sojaka Samuel, Sojane Mxolisi, Soka Zwelibanzi, Sonti Linda Xola, Speedo Dudu, Sukwini Verdict D., Simon, Tafeni Milton, Tanisi Maxwell, Tapi Samson Monwabisi, Tarshish Jack, Tatane Geogre, Tengani Johannes, Thabane Jacob, Thabethe Bhekithemba, Thabethe Charles, Thabethe Solomon, Thejane Joel, Thenjekwayo Nkosinathi, Theo Mkhaliphi, Thile Mark Langa, Thobela Thabo, Thole Mthunzi, Tholo James, Thomas Lungile, Thwala Abraham, Thwala Gwaza, Thwalo Thabo, Timothy Dinasdo Xaba, Tiro Aaron, Tiro Abraham, Titana Themba, Tladi Lazarus, Tsakane Phillip, Tsame Fikile, Tsele Benson, Tshabalala Amos, Tshabalala Fani, Tshabalala Mpini, Tshabalala Vusi, Tsie Joseph Parker, Tsotetsi Stanley, Tuku Thembisile T. Twasi Chiao, Vasi Mzwanele, Velaphi Kenneth, Ventolo Michael, Vilakazi Sipho, Voyi Sizile William, Vundla Jabu, Vundla Patrick S., Wasa Nkululeko, Watts Agnes, Wesi Kenny, Williams Cecil, Winter Bishop Colin, Xaba Timothy Dinamo, Ximba Jacob, Xolo Michael, Xulu Stembiso Walter,Yekiso Sandile, Yende Prudence, Yengwa M.B., Yesiko Sandile Danisile, Zama Maureen, Zami Joe, Ziba, Vuyani, Zikalala Mbusi, Zikhali Artwell, Zondani Mkhuseli, Zondi Basil Amos, Zondi Cassius, Zondo Charlton, Zondo Thomas Petro, Zono Lamula, Zulu Thami, Zungu Funani, Zwelonke Zulu, Thobile Mpumza, Thabiso Thelejane, Anele Mdizeni, Makhosandile Mkhonjwa, Julius Mancotywa, Janeveke Liau, Thabiso Mosebetsane, Mafolisi Mabiya, Ntandazo Nokamba, Fezile Saphendu, "Ngxande" Sitelega Gadlela, Henry Pato, Micheal Ngweyi, Patrick Akhona Jijase, Bonginkosi Yona, Andries Msenyeno, Mzukisi Sompeta, Jackson Lehura, Mphumzeni Ngxande, Mpangeli Lukusa, Mongezeleli

Ntenetya, Cebisile Yana, Mguneni Noki, Khawamare Elias Monesa, Bongani Ndongophele, John Ledingoane, Babalo Mtshazi, Thembinkosi Gwelani, Nkosiyabo Xalabile, Bongani Mdze, Teleng Mohai, Modisaotsile Sagalala, Molefi Ntsoele, Hassan Fundi, Frans Matlhomola Mabelane, Thapelo Eric Mabebe, Tembelakhe Mati, Hendrick Tsietsi Mohene, Sello Ronnie Lepaaka, Sandi Teyise, Mlanduli Hendry Saba, Pumzile Sokanyile, Anene Booysen, Lindiwe Chibi, Francis Rasuge, Karabo Mokoena.

For all our people
For those alive
For those who pray(ed)

Foreword

The 27th of April 1994, the day of South Africa's liberation, marked the triumph of freedom over many years of colonial and apartheid oppression. This epoch-making event was a product of relentless struggles fought by generations of heroes and heroines: fearless warriors who fought in the wars of dispossession; visionaries who dared to dream of an alternative South African society; brave youth and student leaders who took the struggle for liberation to a higher level; determined workers who swelled the ranks of the militant trade union movement and patriotic South Africans, drawn from all races, who led the final push towards the demise of apartheid.

The South African struggle for liberation also drew on the massive support and solidarity of millions of men and women of goodwill across the globe who were single-minded in their mission to bring us our freedom.

The attainment of liberty was the first decisive step in the path of reconstruction and development: a path that sought to harness the life experiences, skills, energies and aspirations of the people of South Africa towards the complete eradication of apartheid and its vestiges, as well as the building of a united democratic, non-racial, non-sexist and prosperous future for all.

Indeed, 1994 brought with it the great promise of economic growth, development and redistribution, social cohesion, reconciliation and nation building, all which were necessary in ensuring that, as a nation, we make a permanent and decisive break with our unhappy past. These were also building blocks towards the South Africa we want.

It is encouraging that twenty-five years later, our freedom and democracy endures. Without fear of contradiction, we can say that much has been achieved since that epoch-making day of April the 27th 1994:today's South Africa is a much better place than 1994's. Our nation has trudged a very long road from an embittered and divided past to a society based on respect for human rights, equality and dignity for all.

However, the road ahead remains long, steep and winding. More needs to be done to translate ur freedom into profound socio-economic change in the lives of many South Africans, to whom the great promise and optimism of 1994 has given way to disappointment and hopelessness.

In this collection of poetry, Lawrence Mduduzi Ndlovu retraces our steps as a nation from the period immediately preceding freedom and democracy in 1994 to where we are 25 years later.

He begins by reminding us that the treasure that is our freedom came at an enormous cost. Many warriors have died for us to be free. Young and old; black and white, men and women have had to give off themselves for us to see the day of freedom. Many prayed for us to be free. Many still pray for our freedom, that it may endure.

Mduduzi causes us to recall the anxiety that accompanied the transition to democracy. He reminds us of the reconciliation hand that the previously oppressed offered to their tormentors.

He writes in one of his opening poems:

"We try call them back
Each time we affirm that they
Wouldn't have been tolerated this lawlessness
We offer our supplications
Direct our libations to them...

In the collection, Mduduzi also speaks of the hope that was ignited in 1994. He refers to this as a *"bright morning [that...] will dispel yesteryear's idleness [...and] win for new pathways, dispelling defeating stagnancy"*. More profoundly, this collection reminds us of the mistakes we have made along our journey as a free people. In what he aptly refers to as "The Turn", Mduduzi speaks of how former comrades – previously united against a clear, identifiable enemy – suddenly found themselves at opposing ends of the new post-1994 divide. In this regards he writes:

Some leaped
For the enemy's chalice
The same one
Stolen from the people
And below their own breath
Whispered to themselves
That it is all mine

Others ran to see
The treasures of the slain beast
Found some things
Then saw that some things
Were already taken
Then turning to each other
Began to see the smug
Of the old enemy
Only this time
On each other's faces

This was the beginning of an era when farewell to comradeship was bade.

Mduduzi proceeds further to reflect on "The Fire" currently engulfing our country. The genesis of this fire is our mistakes and missteps over the past 25 years. It manifests itself in the growing loss of confidence in institutions and leaders by those who feel left behind and ignored:

Patience is one thing
Being ignored is injustice
[...] Being ignored is painful."

The collection ends on a somewhat positive note when Mduduzi writes:

"I believe in one land
Birthing and teeming
Feeding and filling
Giving yet Inexhaustible
Creative and wealthy
I believe in one people
One bark
Different and long adventitious roots
Same fruit
And flowerings of beauty unparalleled.

In leaving the reader with a feeling of hopefulness, Mduduzi reminds us that, even as we face challenges; even as we have made mistakes along our journey; and even as the temptation to believe that there is little hope looms large, we must never give in to pessimism. We are a nation of eternal optimists. We have, many times, triumphed over adversities. We have risen above the odds. We are a resilient people.

At all times we must remember that societies are never static. They are in a constant state of motion. Motion is a necessary condition for progress, as it fuels hope for a better tomorrow.

With visionary leadership, sound policies and strong, credible institutions, the current shifts – the current motion – in our politics and economics can be harnessed for the good of the country.

I commend Father Mduduzi Ndlovu on this wonderful and elaborate collection of poetry. This collection is a useful addition to the body of literature that is helping our nation to critically reflect on its past, while at the same time imagining the future that lies ahead.

Kgalema Motlanthe - October 2019

Preface

There is a permanent longing that many people live with every day. On the one hand, it is a healthy yearning, which causes each person to work harder, to become more than they were yesterday; on the other hand, it is the great sadness of the unfillable void – a complete state of helplessness – because no matter the dream or zeal, the conditions that one finds himself or herself in are not conducive for thriving. The person under the bridge, exposed every day, longs for a place called home. The shack dweller longs for a decent home. The unemployed person longs to dignify his or her life and that of his loved ones with work. The ailing citizen desires only remedy. The woman wants to live in perpetual safety. The intelligent student wants to study but has no money. There are cries for land, both for living and tilling. All these daily pleas often remain unheard, and even when they are heard, they are ignored. Those weeping do so in the presence of those laughing. Those in need do so in the presence of those with plenty.

It seems to me that on this 25th anniversary of our political liberation we are standing not only in a state of longing, but also at the threshold of a paradox. Every day we are walking between life and death, between hope and despair, sadness and joy, rage and excitement. Ours has been a history of great pain and destruction but also of building and bliss. We have moved from hope, and lived through downward turns that felt, and still feel, like avalanches having their descent with unhindered abandon. We have felt and watched this in a state of shock and helplessness, as the country swerved from hope to destruction. These experiences are convoluted: they are one big paradoxical experience for every person in South Africa.

Amidst all these high and low encounters (which often fool many into thinking that they are normal occurrences of all people everywhere) there is a smouldering fire, dusty and grey at the surface, but red and hot underneath, looking dead, but very much alive. It is the same fire that birthed our freedom. It can purify and create. It is also a fire that can be destructive and filled with anger and rage. This nation, standing at this very important threshold, knows well about birthing and dying, about fighting and choosing peace.

We stand at the door of choice. The choice is between continuing with the known or risking the unknown. The known means to continue as we have been doing in the past 25 years. It might sustain us for some time, but it will not hold for long, because it fans the fire in many people. It will come ablaze, it has already begun. As poet William Butler Yeats writes;

Turning and turning in the widening gyre
The falcon cannot hear the falconer;
Things fall apart; the centre cannot hold;
Mere anarchy is loosed upon the world,
The blood-dimmed tide is loosed, and everywhere
The ceremony of innocence is drowned;
The best lack all conviction, while the worst
Are full of passionate intensity.

The unknown is the risk of doing things right , and thus moving into the next phase of our liberation. It is not a blind wondering: it is a different way. It is a way that we all know of, but have chosen not to take. This vision drives all levels of society, and demands everyone to do what they are supposed to do. If teachers teach, health workers heal, students learn, police protect and workers — in whatever profession — work, if politicians bother themselves about proper ethical governance, this new vision can materialise fast.

The choice to title this work *Mayibuye* emerged out of the complex encounters that typify the South African experience. Our struggle has always been one of restoration. In her preface to the book *In Quiet Realm*, Ambassador Lindiwe Mabuza writes: "Slavery took Africans from their land. Colonialism took the land from Africans." Therein one finds the foundations of our unending sense of longing. Those who have been taken from their land are today mere vagabonds, with no place to call home. Those who have lost their land want it back. One can dare not say that the war cry *Mayibuye* is irrelevant to our times. This chant reminds us that there is so much that must be returned to us. 25 years later, we are still not economically free. The great African nations of the past had women as leaders, and women were most respected in the national planning in the family, which was seen as a cultural unit. In order to illustrate this point, one need not go further than reminiscing Mkabayi kaJama, one of the greatest figures in the history of the Zulu nation, or even the roles played by *Makhadzi* in the Venda culture. Somehow, we lost that to a patriarchal system, which is killing all of us, men and women alike. We are not done chanting freedom. Until it is truly within our reach, we shall chant unceasingly... Mayibuye!

Lawrence Mduduzi Ndlovu

Mayibuye

Hear ululations down on earth
The three hundred
and forty two years old enemy
who gripped us and all that is ours
is said to be slain
Is it theirs yet
that Africa our home?
Or are they still wrestling
Jostling as they Shout;
Let it return!
MAYIBUYE!

Tell Me Oliver

Tell me Oliver
what on those mountains
whispered the presence
of something higher
which must be attained?

Need I attune my ear
so I too can hear it
then whisper
that same soothing cheering
to children forgotten
in silent rural homes?

Tell me Oliver
about the pilgrim's song
that said to you
leave now
for beyond
chanting songs of freedom

Tell me Oliver
what on foreign faces
led you to accept as true
that they might believe you
when you spoke
of your people's incarceration
and displacement?

Oh do tell Oliver

how you made the world
sing the same song
birthed with whispers from
rural Nkantolo mountains
and through it
brought the world here
and exiles home

Giants Bow Out

When as a child in state of no worry
napping and unalarmed
giants toiled that their heirs
should never encounter, unarmed
the gruesome glare of regimes that seek to disparage them...

Their true might
was found in the silence of the night
in the their progenies' slumber they strived
carving a future so different
from their belligerent past

They dreamt of an offspring
That would not just toil for toiling's sake
one that would create
not just imagine...
one that would be...

When giants wave goodbye
they turn to their young like a joyous tide
pouring blessings of hope upon sides
their manner astute
their touch gentle
they bid the youth arise!
Arise son!
Arise daughter!
Awaken to maturity!

They must depart

for the torment of the night is gone
Nigh are the flickers of dawn
hopelessness demolished
fear relinquished

Giants depart
for time ascribed has expired
Day is victorious
their battles with night, no more
As they recede, they stand at a distance
like mother & father sparrows to their offspring
"Soar child,
the ceiling has been shuttered"
Like landlords and landladies, they gesture...
"Plough child, the land is now fertile"
Like people's persons they demand...
"Give in, there is abundance for all"

Giants wave goodbye
not too far for their descendants to forget
Nor too near for their regress
They reside in the heroes' balcony
Toasting and singing
with an eye beholding the young
They cheer for every victory
whispering the solution

The young will learn and toil
for when their children awaken
the skies ought to be clear
and the fields fertile

The Handover

Once they were here
their footprints are proof
This freedom we know
was breathed into life
by their own words
it stands upright at their voices

We call them back
each time we claim
they wouldn't have tolerated
this lawlessness

We offer supplications
Direct libations
to hear a whisper:
"It's in your hands now…"

HOPE

Their eyes are of hope's watchful gaze
That maybe this bright morning
Will dispel yesteryear's idleness
And win for new pathways
dispelling defeating stagnancy

Freedom Day

April 1994

Did you see
yesteryear's terrorists?
Tall
with heightened shoulders?
Free
not pardoned,
but self-liberated?

Did you meet the
former stateless
when on tarmac landing?
Regal, walking
to ululations
and benedictions
on home soul?

Did you notice them?
Calm on street bends
amidst smokeless townships?
Yesterday's roadrunners,
now of tomorrow speak
with nothing but hope?

Did you stand
on winding queues
to mark
the leader of your own

choosing not for the living
But winding in procession?
Down that soil
to whisper to those who
died for this choice
"Not in vain, comrades...
Did you die
for here
now
one person
one vote?"

Did you lift
that revolutionary fist?
to validate that power
so long longed for?
It's now with the people
already, but not yet
that clutch of fist
means something
is attained
Power's avalanche
must unfold
will unravel
in its entirety

Did you see the prisoners walk free?
Did you see the living
taking proxy of freedom
even from the slaughtered?
To mark here

freedom dawning
emerge from voting booths
to shout fearlessly
Amandla! Awethu!
Mayibuye! iAfrika!
Izwe lethu! iAfrika!
All Power! To the people!

Here We Stand

The First Democratic Parliament

Said truth to lies
This was never a competition,
it is not about winning
but about how things
are meant to be

Said belief to incredulity
without me
this moment wouldn't be
for the spirit knows
this right must be achieved

Said life to death
Don't you know
that the spirit never dies?
That killing people
does not extinguish their fire?

Said freedom to captivity
they were always free
for they never believed
they were criminals
that bodies can be confined
but
their spirits dance free
growing with joyous abandon

Said peace to war.
They are made for me,
only through me
can beauty be seen,
taste be enjoyed
and silence
and stillness
become the norm

When they walked in
lies scampered at the sight of truth
When they sat down
scepticism gave way to belief
When they stood up
life arose
their presence
was enough to speak of freedom.
And in singular triumphant chorus
Albertina proclaimed for all:
"Mr Chairman I nominate
Nelson Rolihlahla Mandela
For election as President
Thank you"

First Fruits

Colours descended
like sweet matins
on township row

Little feet
crystal eyes
on the first
fresh morning
their journey
towards becoming
started in the New Year

It looked like fun
in parent's hands
until they were set free
into their teacher's hand
Then weeping began
for both parent and child

Old ones
acting like adults
walked steadily
towards the future
of their choice
free from predestined lives
and chains

I saw colours rising
the kids of former servants

being free to choose to be
anything they want

NOTE: I remember that during the apartheid era, we would often wake up to go to school. It always began with hope, until the townships started burning, and we had to be released early or would end up not going to school at all.
My family home is located next to a combined school. I once stood outside the gate, and saw small children being taken to school for the first time. I also saw older kids walking to school on their first day. It was peaceful and hopeful. It was like seeing the rainbow after a storm.

I Prefer It Closed
Truth and Reconciliation Commission

I prefer to see
the door
that separates the now from the then
closed

I prefer it closed
Because I can hear
my sister's screams
behind it

I prefer to see the chamber
from which blood flows endlessly
closed
and I still hear the cries
from the unmarked graves
of my people:
"Take me home
Take me home"

I prefer it closed
the abode
where
for my skin's sake
I was told where to walk
where to work
how to talk
who to be

on my land

I prefer it closed
because I know
what it can reignite
if I am made to open it
so everyone can hear
that legalised evil
once lived here

For all these years of pain
how does my enemy stand
before me with nothing in his hands
begging for my forgiveness
not out of contrition
but for amnesty's sake?
He opens his crimes to me
ripping me bare
daggering me raw
this is no reconciliation

They say let us reconcile
I say I am tired of fighting

How can I reconcile
for reconciliation's sake
when I am still homeless
orphaned
and workless
when I have to live
with my privileged oppressor

still protected by the very laws
my people died for?

This is why
I prefer to see it closed
in my own time
away from confessions
I will learn to trust again

We The People

The Promulgation of the New Constitution 18 December 1996

When the law is unreasonable
the pillars of order give in
protection
falls down
on those who need it

We learnt to separate that day
legal doesn't always mean
good
promulgated ordinance
can serve some
and be a weapon against others

Our struggle was hard
they clicked their fingers
and made us illegal,
their twisted reasoning
legitimised torture

When the law is unreasonable
those charged with safety embody danger
prisons confine the virtuous
thugs rule
protection is heaped
on those already armed

Ours was no struggle

honed out of envy for our oppressor
to win reason back into law
to see us the way we knew ourselves

Clause by clause
we turned previous inversions
right side up
raising her gaze
lady justice
saw what we chanted
we belong here
we the people
we are all equal
we the people!

What happens
when the law becomes reasonable?
it protects all with no discrimination
no one dares to break it
because fighting the law
is like chewing the timber
of the boat you are sailing on

The Builder Knows

When all looks like rubble
the designer's mind will
bring life
out of chaos

Brick by brick
he begins to win from idea
into full reality
he farrows the mud
digging foundations
making them solid

Bit by bit
some new stead
comes alive
through his very hands
sweat, and strength

Building a new country
with fresh ideas
and timeless virtues
to see
new people becoming
what they want to be
out of township rubble
is fulfilling
to see the fighter's prayer answered
is gratifying

Day by day
with steady pace
building the country of our dreams
the home we longed for
not just an idea
trapped in freedom songs anymore...
Here
now
through our own hands
through our own strength...
building...

She Is Learning

She is learning
that her dark skin
is her armour
that wearing the clothes she likes
is fine,
that her costumes
are not barbaric
they tell of the gaiety
of African landscapes
and colourful personalities

She is learning
that her mother tongue
outpours intelligence
her sound
hits the core

When she travels
nothing speaks like home
no one
sings like Africa

She is learning
that conquering the world
means conquering home
that all she needs
is here
in Africa

AUTHOR'S NOTE: Seeing someone wearing a shirt, or dress made of African style fabrics, or beadwork, or an Ndebele neckpiece, or any indigenous motif is commonly accepted today. It was not always so. There was once a shunning of all things tribal and rural. In the minds of some, rural life once symbolised backwardness. This is slowly changing.

Here They Come

When they thought
this new day
would end
with us butchering them
for the crimes they committed
they started running

When they heard no screams
no stories of revenge
they started peeping at the gates
and returning
one by one

When we opened our arms
they made this home of ours
theirs

A festival of blackness
poured into us
shades of black
have made us richer
more complex
more beautiful

If one can risk building a home
in a country he doesn't own
then that place
is the right one
because

they see this land
as a place where they can become
the people they need to be
the ones Africa needs

THE TURN

Sometimes they strew His way
And His sweet praises sing
Resounding all the day
Hosannas to their King
Then "Crucify!"
is all their breath
And for His death
they thirst and cry.

"My Song Is Love Unknown" is a hymn by Samuel Crossman

The Turn

They had a common enemy
their eyes fixed on him
they studied him
lest his mutations
outsmarted him

With hands gripped
on the heavy sword
they took all their might
and struck him down

The enemy is dead!
They rejoiced
and celebrated!
Free at last!

Then they saw
that having a common foe
united them
concealed their own vices
the thuggery hidden silent
in their inmost selves

The ones who
held freedom's sword
loathing everything of their enemy
upon conquering him
began to see
that their motifs

were different

Some leaped
for the enemy's chalice
the one that was
stolen from the people
and below their own breath
whispered to themselves
"It is mine!"

Others ran to see
the treasures of the slain beast
found some things
and saw that others
had already been taken

Turning to each other
they began to see the smug
of the enemy
on each other's faces

Goodbye Comradeship

They stood in corridors
little groups hissing
little serpent's whispers
some seen
others only heard

As he passed,
some waved
smiling as their snake tails
wagged under their pants and frocks

There was a time
when they would jump for joy
at the sight of each other
and the name comrade
meant simply
you are my blood
you are me

Comrade today
could mean "keep him close"
when all their breath
chants:
"Crucify him!
Crucify her!"

Something is dying before us
some being mine
no longer is
some order right
is going wrong

Marikana 2012

On that koppie
my people sat
wanting to be heard
but were killed instead

In that hole
my people descended
day after day
risking their lives
just to feed
their greedy masters who
in turn
gave them crumbs
just enough
to keep them alive
not because they cared for them
but because they needed them
to fill their unfillable guts

Imagine
human life
traded for bread crumbs...

In that town,
they stood
asking for a bit more
pleading to have enough
so that their children
would never

enter the belly of the earth
for leftovers

The mine
the trenches
didn't kill them
The so called humans
did.

Never thought that
a black government
which is meant to know
about slavery
oppression
and mass murder
would
that take away

husbands from wives
fathers from children
brothers from families
just because they dared
to demand what they deserved

Once we detested
the death of our people
at the hands of racists
today
an instruction is given
by our own
to mute our own

That loathsome moment
has turned us inside out
Our filthy hearts
have shouted for all to hear
that nothing
no one
must stand between
our money
and our comfort
that industry is priced
much more than black life

On this land
miners were killed
for daring to ask
for what they deserved

Esidimeni 2016

Saw bodies of the vulnerable today
from the mouths of death dens
and I wondered
how they got there
in the first place

Saw the already weak dead today
after being sacrificed
by the strong
and I wept
at how the strong
could have protected them
but instead
they lowered them into graves

They couldn't speak
when they were shifted
without care
when utter negligence
ate at their flesh
for some
clever beast
couldn't be bothered
by the special care
they needed in order
to stay alive
they were seen
as lesser beings,
and dealt with as such

If they died
they wouldn't be missed
For humanity has been reduced
to production tools

A massacre of the weak
has shown us
that the strong
are cruel
for they can lower their mallets
and bring death
to the defenceless

The Auctioned State

We thought we ruled here
and often shouted
that power was ours

We thought we chose
who led us
and too often
we saluted them
calling them
my leader

Foolish we were
deluded by their grins
while out of our sight
they've been selling
our country
to whoever has
the shiniest coin

I joke not
when I tell you
that they sold
themselves first
now like melting candles
lacking stature
without a semblance of dignity
they scatter their corrupt wax
burning the sturdy surface
so long lathed

polished, and tested
by freedom fighter's blood
all just for greed's sake

They bend to the heat
of their masters brazier
as he so burns them
until they are consumed

We were dressing up
acting like we run this place
while, in reality
we were ceremonial stooges
for a country long sold

What Can Turn Her Back?

What can turn her back?
Could it be the persistent rising of our sun
the absurd offertory of those orange rays
giving unreservedly
until life raises its extremities towards it?

Could it be the mysterious sprouting fields
that uncoil their inmost beauty
exposing their tenderness
whose petals are like outstretched arms?
For the wondering bee to draw sweetness
neither for flora's sake
nor for honey's sake
but for relay of sweet love
one to another

What can turn her back?
Could it be the birthing
that seems to continue
even in death-tide?

Every day is the first day
for some baby crying
in her mother's hand

What can turn her back?
Could it be the recollection
of the lives spent and lost into yesterday's struggle
that cannot be betrayed

for the vanities that coins can give?

What can turn her back?
Could it be the hope that peeps
at the gates of the future?
The past has no final say
because tomorrow it ceases to exist?

It seems to me
that can turn her inwards
is the undeterred ways of nature
which allows to sun to rise each day
which carpets the fields with glorious flowering
which brings forth new life regardless
which ushers the hope we need for tomorrow
Turn again, we implore
Turn the right way around, we beg

THE FIRE

There are some fires
that colour homes cosy
and renders them warm
and in foetus position
some rest beside them
for life is truly good

There is another fire
burning inside many
it is now red blood
ready to set ablaze
the unjust disparities
for life is not good

Patience Is One Thing

Patience is one thing
Being ignored hell
My people sit shuffling
On queues days unending
Only to make the front
Just on time
As shatters descend
And breaks begin

Patience is one thing
Being ignored is painful
See them carry the ill
Sometimes on wheel barrows
On foot
Great distances
Only to find
That the first remedy
Has long dried
From the very havens of health

Patience is one thing
Being ignored is injustice
They say the youth is the future
Yet they put them in mud schools
They die
In pit lavatories
And when the heavenly showers descend
Even the smallest streams
Cannot be crossed

For bridges do not exist
Whether to make it to school
Or to crossover into the future they deserve

Patience is one thing
But being ignored
Is hell
Is pain
Is injustice

The War Is On

The war is still on
it never really ended
Women's bodies are still battlefields
where terror and rage
marks them like wild animals
owned territories
stalked,
guarded like prey

There should be no confusion here
for this circling dance
is not one of protection
but of pure ownership
which aims at nothing but objectifying them
as instruments of pleasure

History
did not teach that no woman
can belong to herself
that she is either her father's daughter
her husband's wife
or a widow in the care of her son.

Does it come as a surprise
that every night
she prays for an armour
that will protect her
lest she becomes another female body
carried out of her home in the morning?

The war is on
the way it was in the cotton fields
under ruthless employ
relentlessly slaving
Because of her gender,
she earns nothing compared
to what the man
sweating besides earns

Tell me these are not war times
for in war
curfews are imposed
women live in a
state of emergency
for no woman
is safe outside herself
She has to plan
every movement
for nothing lets her be
no place is safe enough

The war is still on,
we dare not say to her:
"Rejoice, my dear,
we are free"
What freedom is this
when all about war
Still harasses her?

Africa Apart

Xenophobia

It is not defeated
colonialism is still here
for we look
with grisly eyes
and our mouths
spit vile utterances
because these are no southerners

Someone told us
that we are different
and we believed him
He laughs now
at the height of this foolishness
for too much time
is spent hating
and killing

Let them devour each other
they are better apart
than united
this is why this cradle
our continent,
chooses to beg outside
because she believes that
all things right
cannot be found here

Something is acted out here
and we refuse to talk about it
We think our silence will chase it away
but it's not going anywhere

Volcanoes –
There Still Volcanoes Here #Feesmustfall

Deep inside them
still runs that
fiery lava
and although it is
still their edifice
the piping hot rumbling
still boils like before

These volcanoes
bear names
of slain young lions,
of old ones that roared then as they do now
When the youth's real agency
was undermined
it poured out fire
pelting with their own hands
doors barring them from their future

Was that not why
Hector Peterson
first painted the streets of Soweto red?

Did not those instruments of evil
Seek to cover
the fire of the Tsietsi Mashinini mountain
with their machinations?

Then
and now
young lava shot right back

Hope's Watchful Gaze

Leaning on rocks
fortresses on township bends
another day ends before them
nothingness that typified yesterday
persists today

The youthful steady frame
renounces slumber-filled days
but it's doomed for another day without labour
yet it rises because in its condition
it must work for its own dignity

Their eyes are of hope's watchful gaze
maybe this bright morning
will dispel yesteryear's idleness
and win for new pathways
dispelling defeating stagnancy

See them for the future they are
not roadside hooligans
but dreamers at the margins
of their potential
Their abundance is so close to them
yet the geographies of their birth
the colour of their skin
has already marked them for doom

What is it to be young
if it is not to be a dreamer?

What is it to be strong
if it not to be given space to build?
What is it to be born
if life's purpose cannot be fulfilled?

On Reduced Personhood

No time for dreams here
we live one day-by-day
No space for future dreams
we need enough to stay alive
we are reduced
to beings of survival

Done With Order

He put down his goblet
like ants at the smell of sweetness
My people appeared
wanting to lick the remains
of his pig-style banquet

My people eat spoils
of the bounty they owned
and even then
they are told to do it orderly

Who dare say
to the scavenging beasts of the wild
come in procession
to the carcasses left behind
by the hunters?

But they say
to those reduced to scavenging
that they should wait
their turn is coming
What is due to them
Will be given

A hungry stomach
is not filled by promises
A homeless body
takes shelter wherever it finds it
and dare not be told to wait

What A Joke

I laugh
every time
I hear them say
education will lead you
out of poverty

Where have you heard
a hungry child being told
to read
Before he is fed?

I laugh
when they say:
idling hands
are the devil's tools

But, of course
work awaits me
As soon as I graduate from
the mud school

tell me a better joke
than saying to the youth
that the future is in their hands
as if the future
has been prepared for
by the holders of the now

All I have

as my tool out of depression
is my laughter,
as I watch them
trying to mop the floor dry
while the taps are still running

A Place Called Home
Land

We had homes, remember?
When settlers arrived
and before we could say welcome
we were homeless
and they had our homes

Then we moved about
until we became
labour animals
They built
barnlike dwellings
square by square
and said: you belong here

Four rooms
and often less
could never be enough

We are not getting better
for we moved from land
to tin homes
The thought of what comes
after shacks
is – perhaps - the scariest

Do They Ever Think Of Us?

Solomon Mahlangu:
"My blood will nourish the tree
that will bear the fruits of freedom"

My blood is no seed
of a people unable to see
the hunger of the other
or to heed
the cries for justice
Do you ever think of my blood?
Do you ever think of us?
Tsietsi Mashinini
Ruth First
Chris Hani

What of Tambo
working unceasingly
letting the world know
that his people live with suffering
breaking the façade
isolating the enemy
until he breaks
and freedom beams in?

Hear his voice
could I have missed
my own children's maturing
only for my sweat to become
the bedrock for impunities

corrupt and compromised?
Do they think of my exile?
Do they ever think of us?

Beast In The Wild

There is a beast lurking in the wild
it thinks we don't know it
should we let it prowl
while we study its ways
or lower the bush
so that our pleasantries might tame it?
Should we strike it dead
lest it multiplies
and overpowers us?
Should we show it our strength
so it is reduced by fear?

There is a beast lurking in the wild,
strike it down!
We render ourselves cruel
embrace it!
We are fooled by its odd smile
let it be!
It will never let us be
and so we stare...

Black White Act

The only reason
this black self is accepted
in any edifice of success
is because it sounds white
it acts white
to make the white holders of the purse
comfortable

This racial school
still runs deep
and it shall be so
until the freedom chanted
is one with the freedom lived

In the meantime
blacks are still poor
and whiteness still means privilege

Democracy

This Democracy
Is tough
Truth is
We can't take it
But we need it
Truth is
It is ambitious
Truth is
We need protection
We have a right to be here

STILL WORTH LOVING
Still Here

There's still something here
that refuses to go
as some board ships,
and it claims this place
is home no more...
I watch it
to remember
that this
is the only home I know

Still Alive

This place
Is alive
with a rhythmic heartbeat
beat after beat

That is why
even in the early morning
the sangoma's drum
makes feet stump at the pulse
beads chanting at every stump
blood flowing
robed in red,like the sun

See the majorette
twirling her baton
at the bass drum
and the white-gloved brass player
marching right behind her
the smooth gentlemen
hand in hand
with the sassy mshozas of old
tap their perfect shoes
as jazz joins the pulse

Every Sunday afternoon
Heaven is called out
be it by call to prayer
or robed in church vestures

They sing
until, in complete trance
taken over by life
for this place is no home for death
it is alive

Laughter Is Their First Home

Laughter is their first home
a nod to the joy within
gloom may abound
yet it doesn't reach their inner glee

Pass the shack dwellings
where faces should sag
for life hasn't been easy
but laughter is there
rides higher than
the low tins
they have come to call home

They laugh
even amidst absurdity
when fools take to platforms
they are dragged down
put in their place
and laughed at

They laugh at themselves
they bring that out of each other
so their flaws become light
knowing they can start again
Laughter is their home
and home is laughter's abode
It has never left them

Dream It Be It

There was a time
when willing a dream
could never be realised
You could be intelligent
and have no worry about means
but no would be the answer

Now is a time
when willing a dream
can be realised
if you have the intelligence.
Even though means might be a worry
you can work towards your dream
for the time for yes is here

Something has shifted
one's dreams are attainable
no colour can dictate destiny
there might be other hindrances
but who you are is no boundary
anymore

Young Adult

Look at her with more sympathy
sometimes she walks tall
and walks with older friends
holding her own
but she is just a 25-year-old child

Cheeky
to point at her flaws
as if she has a reference
a precedence to learn from

She is no seraphim
but at least she hasn't lived
through two world wars
in her young years
She is no weakling
but the thought of
annexing her sometimes weak neighbours
has never crossed her mind

It must have taken
more than twenty five years
to build an adult state
so why must this young adult
grow faster
just to make everyone
think she is something different
from what she truly is?

It Is Coming

We celebrate
the first black
the first woman
the first black woman
the youngest person
soon phrases will be completed
not to be heard again
it will not be worth celebrating
it will be normal
it is coming

It Is Fine

I believe
my creed is protected
I love
I am free to love
I think
I am free to speak my mind
I exist
I have a right to be here
I belong
I stand with those who stand with me

No point in apologising
for my faith
for loving
for my thoughts
for my association
for my being here

What Still Raises Us

I know what still raises us up
whether the sun rises or not
even without the promise
of tomorrow's benefit...
What still raises us
is that we are not over
the joy of savouring
the fact of our posture
that who we are
does not rely on what the other
thinks we are not...

It's a step worth celebrating
for the first step toward self-emancipation
is the knowledge that
I am adequate
Because of this
I need not prove myself
in order to have what is truly mine

The Rule

You may speak
they said
while sitting
under the big tree...
Grey-haired elders
seated attentively
as the story was retold
with every detail heard
while others sat
around the elders
as justice unfolded
when the sun
was in fullest form

Eleven Seats

sit half-moon shaped
secure
each seat a vote
eleven gates
into justice

They are final
for they never sleep
counting every word
guarding every phrase

They gesture
to anyone who appears
before them
to stand
confidently
armed with full rights
to accuse
or to defend themselves

The book of defence
under their care
lock and key
is brought out

The law is read
in voices of thunder
and chiselled on concrete
Never to be removed

It has always been in us
from times long gone
from under tribal trees
everyone has a right
to be heard...
No mystery, then,
that the court
high on the hill
is for us all
and many beyond
the pinnacle
the measure
of how law
ought to be done

Don't Get Confused

Don't confuse our laughter with timidity
remember the slaves didn't call you boss
because you owned them
they kept up the act
in order to survive

Don't confuse our greetings for fear
it is our way of acknowledging humanity
human should see human
we accompany the one hand with the other
not because the one greeted is greater than us
but because we show that people should
always be met with attention

Don't mistake our saying please
as an invitation to attack as you please
try falling on a porcupine and see
its spikes will stand with ease
and you'll be dealt with thoroughly...

Our forebears tolerated much
because their lives were held cheap
and at gun point they could be vanquished
but we fear no such thing,
get with the times
and get it straight
The timid "Yes Ma'am"
and the shy "Yes bass" are gone
Talk to me

let's agree
I am no servant
nor are you, my Lord
I work with you
not for you
I have my duties
and you have yours
we are trading here
I use my intellect
my time
my strength
You, in turn,
do your part
and pay for my services

African Credo

I believe in one Africa
A united state of being
Honed by the very dust
From north(est) peak
To the south most deep
Whose left arm
Knows the reach of its right
I believe in one cradle
Mother of all
Human
Element
Stone
Water
Fire

I believe in one land
Birthing and teeming
Feeding and filling
Giving yet inexhaustible
Creative and wealthy

I believe in one people
One bark
Different and long adventitious roots
Same fruit
And flowerings of beauty unparalleled

I believe in Africa
Infinite

All ages belong to her
Always has been
Always is her time